WE BOTH READ®

Parent's Introduction

Whether your child is a beginning reader, a reluctant reader, or an eager reader, this book offers a fun and easy way to encourage and help your child in reading.

Developed with reading education specialists, **We Both Read** books invite you and your child to take turns reading aloud. You read the left-hand pages of the book, and your child reads the right-hand pages—which have been written at one of six early reading levels. The result is a wonderful new reading experience and faster reading development!

You may find it helpful to read the entire book aloud yourself the first time, then invite your child to participate the second time. As you read, try to make the story come alive by reading with expression. This will help to model good fluency. It will also be helpful to stop at various points to discuss what you are reading. This will help increase your child's understanding of what is being read.

In some books, a few challenging words are introduced in the parent's text, distinguished with **bold** lettering. Pointing out and discussing these words can help to build your child's reading vocabulary. If your child is a beginning reader, it may be helpful to run a finger under the text as each of you reads. Please also notice that a "talking parent" ☺ icon precedes the parent's text, and a "talking child" ☺ icon precedes the child's text.

If your child struggles with a word, you can encourage "sounding it out," but keep in mind that not all words can be sounded out. Your child might pick up clues about a word from the picture, other words in the sentence, or any rhyming patterns. If your child struggles with a word for more than five seconds, it is usually best to simply say the word.

Most of all, remember to praise your child's efforts and keep the reading fun. After you have finished the book, ask a few questions and discuss what you have read together. Rereading this book multiple times may also be helpful for your child.

Try to keep the tips above in mind as you read together, but don't worry about doing everything right. Simply sharing the enjoyment of reading together will increase your child's reading skills and help to start your child off on a lifetime of reading enjoyment!

About Bats

A We Both Read Book

Level K–1

_____

With special thanks to Alicia Goode at the California Academy of Sciences
for her review and recommendations on the material in this book

We Both Read® is a trademark of Treasure Bay, Inc.

Published by Treasure Bay, Inc.
P.O. Box 119
Novato, CA 94948 USA

Printed in Singapore

Library of Congress Catalog Card Number: 2012938788

Hardcover ISBN: 978-1-60115-267-1
Paperback ISBN: 978-1-60115-268-8

We Both Read® Books
Patent No. 5,957,693

Visit us online at:
www.WeBothRead.com

PR-11-13

WE BOTH READ®

About Bats

By Sindy McKay

With illustrations by Wendy Smith

TREASURE BAY

 Meet Brownie. **She** was born just six weeks ago. **She** can already take care of herself.

 **She** is a bat.

Some people think bats are birds, but they are mammals. You are a mammal too. So is a dog. What else is a mammal?

 A cat!

Why do people think bats are birds? Maybe it's because they have wings and they can **fly**.

Brownie's wings look like four "fingers" with skin stretched between them.

She can **fly**.

During the summer, Brownie lives under the roof of a barn. She lives there with many other mother bats and babies.

It is hot.

In the winter, it gets cold. Brownie and other bats fly south to hibernate, or "sleep," in a cave. In the cave, it is not **too** cold and . . .

. . .not **too** hot.

Brownie wakes up in the spring. She flies back to the same barn where she was born. All grown up now, she has a baby of her own.

It is a pup.

Brownie is one kind of bat. There are many others.

This is a Malayan flying fox. When he spreads his wings, he is about six feet wide.

He is big.

This is a Kitti's hog-nosed bat. He is sometimes called the bumblebee bat. Can you guess why?

He is not big.

 Brownie is a type of bat called a little brown bat. When she spreads her wings, she is about ten inches wide.

Is she big?

Most bats are nocturnal. This means they sleep in the day and come out at night. That makes some people think bats like Brownie are blind, but she is not.

She can see.

Brownie comes out at night to hunt for food. She **eats** moths, wasps, beetles, gnats, mosquitoes, midges, and mayflies.

She **eats** bugs.

Brownie catches her dinner using echolocation. She sends out a noise. It bounces off a bug and comes back to her **ears**. That tells her where the bug is.

She has big **ears!**

Flying fox (also called fruit bat)

Insects are Brownie's favorite food, but some bats eat other things. Flying fox bats fly off at night to eat fruit from **trees**. During the day, they often sleep hanging upside down . . .

Flying foxes (also called fruit bats)

 . . . in the **trees**.

The California leaf-nosed bat eats large insects like crickets, grasshoppers, and even caterpillars. **Some** bats eat lizards, frogs, birds, and rodents.

**Some** eat fish.

Some bats do not eat at all. Vampire bats drink their meals. They bite and drink blood from other animals. They only take a little bit of blood at a time from animals like birds and deer . . .

 . . . and goats.

After Brownie finishes feeding on insects at night, she heads back to her home to rest and sleep. Bats usually sleep hanging upside down by their **feet**.

Head down . . .

. . . **feet** up!

Most farmers like bats like Brownie. Bats help keep mosquitoes and other insects out of our orchards, fields, and gardens.

Bats help us.

Some people even build special houses that bats **like** so that bats will live near them.

Brownie and her family . . .

 . . . **like** it!

Wrinkled-lipped bats exiting a cave at dusk

Of course, not everyone likes bats. Maybe that's because they never learned about bats. Now, you can explain to them how interesting and helpful bats can be. You may even say, . . .

. . ."I like bats!"

Fun Facts About Bats!

Bats live on every continent in the world except Antarctica.

Bats are the only mammals that can fly.

Bats have four fingers and a thumb. The thumb is a small, hook-like nail at the top of the wing. It is used for clinging and climbing.

Most bats are nocturnal. This means they sleep during the day and come out at night.

Bats usually have only one baby at a time.

The Malaysian flying fox is the world's biggest bat. Kitti's hog-nosed bat is the world's smallest bat.

Learn More About Bats!

Parents: If your child is interested in learning more about bats, here are two other books and a website that you might want to look at together.

Bats (National Geographic Kids) by Elizabeth Carney

Bats! Strange and Wonderful by Laurence Pringle

www.batcon.org (website active at time of publication)

If you liked **About Bats,** here is another
We Both Read® Book you are sure to enjoy!

About Dogs

Designed to be read with very beginning readers, this book features fun information about the world's most popular pet. The book covers some of the breeds and some of the special ways dogs help us, including serving as rescue dogs and guide dogs. With great photos and interesting facts, it is sure to be a favorite with anyone who loves dogs!

To see all the **We Both Read** books that are available,
just go online to www.WeBothRead.com